SandCastle

Healthy Habits

Keeping Your Body Clean

Mary Elizabeth Salzmann

Consulting Editor, Diane Craig, M.A./Reading Specialist

ABDO
Publishing Company

Published by ABDO Publishing Company, 4940 Viking Drive, Edina, Minnesota 55435.

Credits
Edited by: Pam Price
Curriculum Coordinator: Nancy Tuminelly
Cover and Interior Design and Production: Mighty Media
Photo Credits: BananaStock Ltd., Corbis Images, Creatas, Digital Vision, Image 100, ImageState, PhotoDisc, Stockbyte

Library of Congress Cataloging-in-Publication Data

Salzmann, Mary Elizabeth, 1968-
    Keeping your body clean / Mary Elizabeth Salzmann.
        p. cm. -- (Healthy habits)
    Includes index.
    Summary: Explains in simple language the importance of keeping our bodies clean and wearing clean clothes.
        ISBN 1-59197-553-0
        1. Hygiene--Juvenile literature. 2. Health--Juvenile literature. [1. Hygiene, 2. Health.]
I. Title.

RA777.S323 2004
613'.4--dc22
                                                                    2003057792

SandCastle™ books are created by a professional team of educators, reading specialists, and content developers around five essential components that include phonemic awareness, phonics, vocabulary, text comprehension, and fluency. All books are written, reviewed, and leveled for guided reading, early intervention reading, and Accelerated Reader® programs and designed for use in shared, guided, and independent reading and writing activities to support a balanced approach to literacy instruction.

Let Us Know

After reading the book, SandCastle would like you to tell us your stories about reading. What is your favorite page? Was there something hard that you needed help with? Share the ups and downs of learning to read. We want to hear from you! To get posted on the ABDO Publishing Company Web site, send us e-mail at:

sandcastle@abdopub.com

SandCastle Level: Transitional

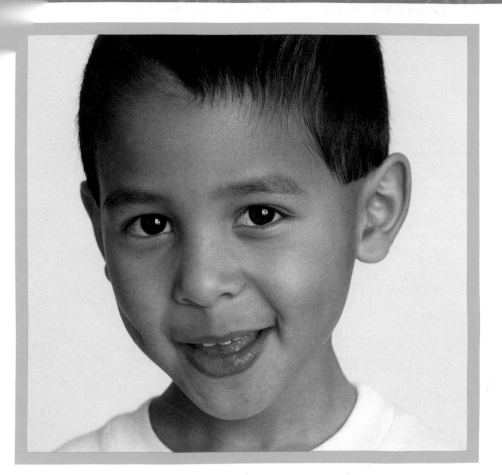

Keeping your body
clean is a healthy habit.

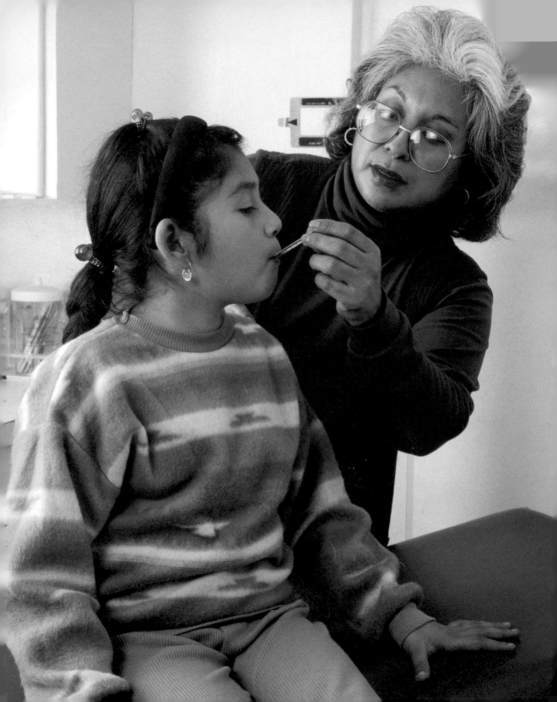

Having a clean body helps prevent germs from making you and other people sick.

You also feel better when your body is fresh and clean.

You keep your body clean by taking a bath or shower every day.

It is also important to wash your hands often so you won't spread germs.

Wearing clean clothes and keeping your hair neat are also part of having a clean body.

Zach likes to play with a rubber duckie in the bath.

Lori brushes her hair until all of the tangles are out.

Jerry helps his mom do the laundry so they will have clean clothes to wear.

What do you do to
keep yourself clean?

Did You Know?

In Pennsylvania it used to be against the law to take a bath more than once a month.

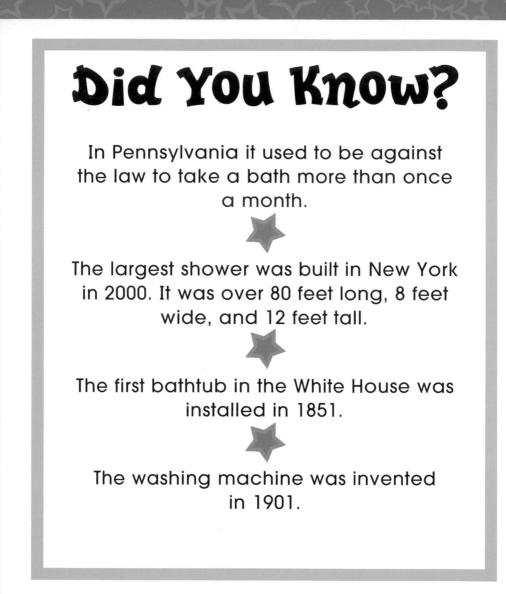

The largest shower was built in New York in 2000. It was over 80 feet long, 8 feet wide, and 12 feet tall.

The first bathtub in the White House was installed in 1851.

The washing machine was invented in 1901.

Glossary

germ. a tiny, living organism that can make people sick

habit. a behavior done so often that it becomes automatic

healthy. preserving the wellness of body, mind, or spirit

laundry. clothes and linens that have been or are being washed

shower. a bath taken under a spray of falling water; the place where you take a shower

tangle. a twisted, knotted mass; a snarl

About SandCastle™

A professional team of educators, reading specialists, and content developers created the SandCastle™ series to support young readers as they develop reading skills and strategies and increase their general knowledge. The SandCastle™ series has four levels that correspond to early literacy development in young children. The levels are provided to help teachers and parents select the appropriate books for young readers.

Emerging Readers
(no flags)

Beginning Readers
(1 flag)

Transitional Readers
(2 flags)

Fluent Readers
(3 flags)

These levels are meant only as a guide. All levels are subject to change.

To see a complete list of SandCastle™ books and other nonfiction titles from ABDO Publishing Company, visit **www.abdopub.com** or contact us at:

4940 Viking Drive, Edina, Minnesota 55435 • 1-800-800-1312 • fax: 1-952-831-1632